The
Shadow Beside Me

ISBN: 978-0-9967409-1-3 (paperback)

Published in December 2020, by

PONGO PUBLISHING, INC.
153 14th Ave, #5
Seattle, WA 98122

www.pongoteenwriting.org
programmanager@pongoteenwriting.org

Cover Art: Mario Avalos
Book Design: Dania Zafar
Editor: Shaun Anthony McMichael

Photo credit (Cover and pp. 5, 25, 47, 59, 73)
Jungle Gym © Akintevs/iStock.com

Printed and bound in the United States of America

The
Shadow Beside Me

**PONGO POETRY FROM
KING COUNTY JUVENILE
DETENTION**

Founder:
Richard Gold

Executive Director:
Barbara Green

Development Manager:
Nebeu Shimeles

Program Manager:
Shaun McMichael

Project Leaders:
Arlene Naganawa, Amani Sawari,
Emily Holt, Emily Caris, Eli Hastings

Poetry Mentors:
Unna Kim, Raúl Sanchez, Nadia Imafidon,
Mark Johnson, Kiana Davis, Sara Jones,
Natalie Singer-Velush, Becky Sherman,
Phaedra Pascoe, Kathleen Levine,
Christy Abram

PONGO POETRY PROJECT
Seattle, WA, December 2020

OTHER BOOKS OF PONGO TEEN POETRY

Dedicated to all of the Pongo teen writers, and to Richard Gold, Pongo's Founder and Executive Director for 25 years.

Thanks to the following grantors for their generous support of the Pongo Poetry Project and this publication:

4 Culture; City Of Seattle, Office Of Arts & Culture; Fales Foundation Trust; Ibis Foundation Of Arizona; Jeffris Wood Fund; Moccasin Lake Foundation; National Endowment For The Arts; Onefamily Foundation; Tulalip Tribes Charitable Fund; Washington State Arts Commission; Angelo Grosso; Kaitlin Mcmichael; Donna And John Riley; R. Dustin Lane

The authors in this book are not identified by their real names. Details in the writing have also been changed to protect the privacy and confidentiality of our authors and their families.

CONTENTS

FOREWORD

RICHARD GOLD, FOUNDER
Pongo Poetry Project

A FEW YEARS AGO I WAS WORKING WITH A YOUNG WOMAN IN JUVENILE detention, where Pongo has served for over 20 years. The environment was notable for the heavy metal doors, loud locks, stained linoleum floors, and thick glass walls that looked out to detention staff posted in the hallway. The young woman had never written before, and we were struggling to come up with a topic, when I suggested we imagine a set of doors in her heart. She dictated a poem in which we opened each door to discover her personal loneliness, frustration, jealousy, terror, and a complicated jumble of hate and love. She ended the poem with;

> Somewhere in there is the perfect life
> A perfect me

This turned into a unique and beautiful poem, but also something greater.

As you read the poetry in this volume, and appreciate its power and artistic merit, I hope you will appreciate the context even more. I am not talking about the context of the detention center, I am talking about the fact that the poetry is the product of opening the doors in one's heart.

This opening is a process of exposing and articulating our painful truths, especially our childhood trauma. The youth in detention are primarily youth of color who have been exposed as children to violence and community dysfunction that result from society's long history of racial oppression. Unfairly, the impact of this childhood trauma on young people is that often it leaves them in doubt about their own worth.

Fortunately, an understanding of our personal pain, as accomplished through poetry, can explain to us who we are and what we can be. It honors our resilience and points us toward finding meaning, including finding purpose through compassion and in action for social change. It helps us to become whole.

I am using the word "us" intentionally. We all struggle with those closed doors in our hearts, and with facing uncomfortable truths in our own lives, including in our roles with others and in social justice. In Pongo's poetry process, the writing mentors, like me, will bear witness to our writers' pain. The youth become our guides on a journey of transformative openness. Pongo's staff, volunteers, allies, and collaborators can all attest to their personal evolution through this work.

Writing this Foreword is an especially poignant opportunity for me, as I have just retired after 25 years of founding and leading the Pongo Poetry Project. I am proud that Pongo has helped so many people, including nationally and internationally. Trauma-informed arts are not only the most humane response to society's problems but the most sensible response. I look forward to the difference Pongo can make in the future.

Finally, I am grateful that the Pongo process and our writers' openness have helped me to become a better human being.

Richard Gold, Founder
Pongo Poetry Project

PREFACE

SHAUN ANTHONY MCMICHAEL

IN THESE POEMS, YOUTH WRITERS LEAD US THROUGH A strange playground. We see the trappings of normal childhood—a backpack, a hula-hoop, a teddy bear. But gunshots ring out, protectors turn abusive, and loved ones don't come home. The children internalize a feeling of worthlessness from these experiences, and this feeling is amplified by widespread social inequality along racial lines created by oppressive systems. In these hostile environments, children develop survival strategies, both creative and self-destructive. Behaviors used to survive in one context often lead them to breaking the law in another, which leads to where they've come to reside: Seattle's Children and Family Justice Center (CFJC), formerly King County Juvenile Detention—where we meet them.

Since 1998, staff and volunteers at the Pongo Poetry Project have been writing with teenagers here. Through collaboration with the school and staff inside the facility, our small teams of trained adult volunteers, called Poetry Mentors, facilitate personal poetry with youth. The majority of them are youth of color. Most don't consider themselves writers. In fact, their pasts are often too terrible for words; when awful memories intrude without warning, their thoughts freeze up, their emotions overwhelm, and problematic behaviors arise from their distress.

With this in mind, Pongo Poetry Mentors invite youth into the world of self-expression with gentleness and support. We ask them what's on their mind. We ask them to try a fill-in-the-blank activity with an evocative, but unobtrusive theme (e.g., Ten Reasons to Love Me (50); I am Old and New (69); The Lessons of Courage and Fear (72). We listen without judgment or agenda while scribing youth responses and asking them follow up questions like "would you like to say more?". Guided by our thoughtful, trauma-informed approach and their courageous drive to tell their stories, youth open up.

Even after recounting events of extraordinary sadness or horror, teens feel a mixture of regret, pride, and relief. With a Poetry Mentor's help, they have encapsulated their experience into a poem, which, unlike the past, has a defined form with a beginning and an end. Unlike some of the most traumatic moments of their lives in which they had no control, youth authors can choose whether or not to share their poems.

Fortunately, these 53 youth authors have chosen to share these poems with you. The title *The Shadow Beside Me* is taken from one young woman's poem describing her past: "all I see is a shadow sitting right next to me" (26). In her poem, the past is hellish and inescapable. In other poems, the idea of the shadow shifts into a presence youth find themselves learning from, and even befriending. This "befriending the shadow" is a guiding metaphor for this collection. Youth authors use poetry to work through profound losses, loneliness, traumatic experiences, and complicated memories of caregivers and communities. In embracing their shadows, their pasts, and their difficult feelings, youth show us how to become more ourselves.

Despite the heart-rending content of their poetry, youth survey results from Detention, and elsewhere report that their writing process with Pongo is overwhelmingly positive:

- 99% enjoy the writing experience, despite 39% being new to poetry
- 98% feel proud of their work

- 73% write about things they normally don't talk about
- 81% felt better after writing

These results are possible because of Pongo's methodology, the openness and courage of the youth, and the skill and dedication of Pongo's community members. This includes not only Pongo's project leads and mentors, but also our friends at CFJC, past and present: Allen Nance (current Juvenile Division Director), Quanetta West (Assistant Division Director), Pam Jones (former Director), Karen Kinch (Volunteer Coordinator), Lynn Valdez (former Supervisor), Unna Kim (Recreational Therapist), Jim Leighty, Marcy Pareira, and Reina Galvez (Mental Health Staff), and Dr. Eric Trupin and Dr. Mick Storck (Psychiatrists and Pongo Advocates). We also want to thank other collaborating organizations inside Detention, Seattle Public Schools and King County Library, and their staff—Stacy Vida (teacher), Thomas Morrow (teacher), and Jill Morrison (librarian).

These poems are a sample of the 900 poems facilitated by Pongo at King County Juvenile Detention from Fall 2015-Spring 2020. The authors' names and some details in their poetry have been changed to protect their identities.

If reading this collection moves you to get involved, there are several ways you can join Pongo in this work.

- Download free writing activities and submit poetry on our website, *www.pongoteenwriting.org*
- Learn about training and volunteer opportunities by emailing *programmanager@pongoteenwritring.org*
- Buy a copy of Founder Richard Gold's book, *Writing with At-Risk Youth: The Pongo Teen Writing Method* (Rowman & Littlefield Education, 2014), a field guide to starting a poetry writing project.
- Donate by visiting our website or emailing *developmentmanager@pongoteenwriting.org*

We know you will find the work worth the challenge. Through this work, we have heard painful stories that we can never forget; yet we feel a fuller sense of humanity and gratitude having heard them. As a young man in this collection writes,

"hurt is a thing—a feeling
that made me who I am today
and it's hurt
I want to thank"
(36).

What We're Made of

Two Different Lives of Pain

There's just something you will never understand.
Like what it feels like to be on heroin and meth,
thinking everything will be ok if you get addicted
because of others around you
and you feel like nobody cares about you anyway
until you die.

There are just some things you will never understand.
Like when you feel the need to sell yourself
for one hundred dollars
because you can get a gram of heroin for forty
and still be ok for the night moneywise.

There are just some things you will never understand.
Like worrying where you're going
to lay your head at night
or who's walking behind you
because people are out to hurt you.

There are just some things you will never understand.
Like feeling your own mother wants you in jail.
But you know it's only to save you,
give you time to talk to God
and find yourself again.

There are just some things you will never understand.
Like feeling held hostage
to something that feels so good
but will kill you in the long run.

There are just some things you will never understand.
You can live two different lives
with two different names
like Superman.
But instead of saving Lois Lane
you need to save yourself.

Dedicated to my mom

It's Hard to Let Go

I can be stronger than an addiction,
ready to say *No,*
I can't surround myself with you.

I can be strong as the winds blowing on a rainy day.
Pay attention to my determination.
If I'm gonna stop,
I'm gonna stop and not do it again.

I'm addicted to people around me.
Sometimes, you know, you gotta let people go
because they're not bettering your future.
I will say *no* to them.
I can be strong in ways you don't expect.

It's hard to let people go, you know.
My co-defendants—
got three in here.
I got associates
and then I got people I call brothers and sisters.
They want me to change.
My associates –
they encourage me:
Fight, fight, fight.

Sometimes, you know, you gotta let family go
because they're not doing their job.
If you're family
you're supposed to be encouraging me to do better.
You know how they say blood is thicker than water?
Sometimes water is thicker than blood.
I have blood that's not family
and I got family that's not blood.

It's hard to let go, you know.
Say stealing.
I can do it again and again and again.
The more times you do something,
the more times you can get caught.

I can be stronger than a mother letting her kids go
and getting off drugs.
I can be stronger than my mom.
It's been so long.
Sometimes, you know, you gotta let mom go.
But not forever —
just until she gets clean.

Dedicated to my family

I Am Made From

People say we are made up of sand or water.
I am made from a dad with lots of smiles and laughs.
We wear the same size genes—
size funny and caring.
I am made from a mom—
the natural to my beauty,
the curly to my lashes, the dimple to my cheek,
the feisty to my attitude.
My mom is far
but when I look in the mirror, I see her.
When I look in the mirror, I see Dad
because I have my dad's eyes.

I am made from the G in grateful,
the I in independence.
I am here, I am alive,
I can do everything by myself.
I am made from black and white.

I am made from being able
to put myself in someone else's shoes.
Regardless if they're too big or too small,
I can still make them fit.

I am made up of teachings that God loves me,
that he'll never leave me, nor forsake me,
to love one another.
They are the reason why
I am able to breathe the clean air
and see the luscious, bright trees,
the sunny-side-up sun.

My dad is the right side
and my mom is the left side.
As much as they may not think so,
they form a heart.
Without them,
I wouldn't have one.

PTSD

It's a child screaming for help
while nobody comes to the rescue.

It's the sound of punching,
like the knuckles hitting bone.

It's someone lying on a bed looking up,
watching it happen to them.
The person who was doing the punching
was listening to Eminem beforehand
and the music pissed them off.

They wondered how to get their anger out
but coming to no conclusions,
paced toward the child.

It's the smell of sweat off the person punching.
It's the feeling of pain,
just a lot of pain—
enough to make them bleed,
enough to leave a bruise.

The child covers their face to protect,
and the person punching
moves from the face
down to the lower extremities.
The child is wishing for it to stop,
hoping for help.

Dedicated to my past self

Wake Up

I wake up to the sound of your voice in my head,
like the way you say good morning
running through my room, making noise
screaming, "Daddy wake up, Daddy wake up."
You with curly hair in a mess,
your sister with her beautiful green eyes
still in her onesie.

I wake up here,
expecting your playful laughter.
Instead,
there is dead silence.

Here
I look in the mirror in the morning wishing
I could hear your footsteps running towards me.
When you would grab a string of floss
and stare at me in the reflection of the mirror,
you would always argue, and I would argue back.
I'm still missing your presence,
even though it's only been a week or two.

I call you after my first meal of the day,
wishing that 15-minute talk time was hours.
I hate having to lie to you
about where I am
but the place I am now
is not a place a girl should know her father is.

Dedicated to my little girl

Living Forever

I live with my grandma and grandpa
because my mom and dad are in prison.

My grandma is really protective.
She watches the news a lot and is afraid
that I am going to be on the news next.

I have this theory that I am going to live forever.
Grandma knows it's not true,
but I keep it in the back of my head just in case.

I had this dream
that me and some friends stole this car,
and we got into a crash.
My head hit the dashboard.

I was looking down at the concrete.
No bruises, no scratches, no nothing.
The car was totaled.
Kids in the car had blood coming from their heads,
broken arms, dislocated shoulders,
but I was fine.

Grandma prays for me every time I leave the house.
I don't take it for granted,
but it just seems normal to me.
I have this theory that I am going to live forever.

Night After Night

I remember those hard-ass nights
when my mom's coming in after a couple's night.
I be already in bed
but that don't mean she should leave.
Just a shorty, only 12-years-old.
Never knew how to cook, so I never touched the stove.
Always had hand-me-downs.
I couldn't afford no clothes.
Sometimes mom thought about it
and start crying all alone.
So, I vowed one day that struggle
would soon be over.

I got older and smarter, grew away from my father.
All he seemed to do was make my life harder.
Started running with people, and my heart—
it got darker.

They helped me turn heartless.
We was savages,
not caring about right or wrong.
Man, screw a consequence!
Living life like an action flick...
It's all gonna come to an end.

I often wonder when my generation gonna stop,
but I be a hypocrite if I said it's easy to stop.

Only thing that comes to mind,
"Keep your head up, shorty."
I know it can be hard, but we all go through it,
but it's time for change.
You can't always be ruthless.

Sweet Wine

I'm from a street
where gunshots at night is nothing new.
People always wonder why the police come through.
Abandoned projects and boarded up houses,
unsupervised children running like mice,
drug dealers and gang bangers
but this isn't new to me.

My household is nothing like what I make it seem.
I make it seem to be what every kid wants
but in reality,
my dad is dead, my mom has breast cancer,
my brother is dead.
But I tell people my life is just fine,
good like sweet wine.

I live in an apartment with my stepdad.
Broken picture frames, holes in the wall
from people slamming doors open.
Roaches scatter when the lights turn on.
Sometimes the water is turned off
from the bill not being paid.
I support myself.

I'm a 20-year-old trapped in a 16-year-old body.
I hang with older people, do older people activities
and festivities—play basketball, smoke,
and people still think I'm a joke.
I feel like I'm grown sometimes
but I know I'm just a child.

Once my dad died, I had no father figure.
My stepdad doesn't care what I do.
In and out of foster care,
been through and made it out
of many group homes.
But then again
people think my life is good like sweet wine.

Dedicated to my brothers

Totem Pole

My mistakes and what happened
Reasons why I'm here
Thinking about the past to the present
Trying to figure out how it began
How it's going to end

My dad's stuck in prison for life without parole
My mom is back on drugs
My brothers are in foster care
I've been homeless for three years

I look at the same totem pole every day
I think about the stories I've heard
There's a man and a woman
back to back
They have each other's backs
no matter what situation they go through

None of my family has each other's back
We always go against each other
I don't get it
I can't go a single day
without being locked up or chased down

I live behind the totem pole in a park
It's like a black hole
You can't ever leave it. There's no way out
Stuck there till the end
I've watched people get hurt, die, never leave
I hear stories about people
who spend their lives there

I keep watch after everyone that lives there
all the natives
making sure no one defaces the totem pole
Now that I'm not there, everything gets bad
When I'm not there, somebody gets hurt

My spirit animal is a black wolf
I have dark sides
that people don't see

Everywhere I go, there's life and death
There's always a shadow on me
stopping me from seeing the light
Hopefully, the shadow will arise
so I can see the light

Dedicated to my family

Until Life is Beautiful Once More

Chicago on the South Side

Everybody should know that when I was younger
at school one day, I went straight from lunch to recess
My brother was driving down the street
Somebody was shooting at his car
The police said that one of the bullets
went through the window
and hit him in the back of his head
He lost control of his car
and crashed into the monkey bars
He opened his door and leaned out
He was just dead
I started crying
They were telling me to calm down
I was shocked to the point where I couldn't think
like I was dying too
I was trying to go to the car
They said I couldn't
Then my mom picked me up from school

Ever since then
I started skipping school
I just didn't want to come no more
because I didn't know what was going to happen there

After that day
that's when I started changing
I can't lead the life that I started
That happened 4 years ago
When you know you can't get somebody back
When you can't even walk up to them
or give 'em a hug
you feel empty like an alley
that leads to a big field
like an endless row with nothing there

Home vs. Juvenile

Home is watching my little brother and sister
It's playing games, it's cooking
Home feels like...*damn*
It don't feel like Juvenile. It don't
Home feels like sleeping
more comfortable than the beds here
Home is freedom
I get to go outside and come back in
I get to help my little brother and sister
I be talking more at home
I be going outside, playing basketball with friends
You don't get to have friends in your cell here
Home is where I get to have fun
I tell myself: *go outside, go outside*
Have hella fun, come back whenever you want

Here is hell
I just smell toilets
I just look at white
I don't see anything but my wall & my book
The only thing I see outside is dirty stuff
Dirty grass, trees with no leaves, fences
A building covering the city
I just see two doors, one bathroom, the stairs

When I'm at home
I be seeing good stuff, clean stuff
My room, my house
My living room
I see my mom's face

My Dad

I miss my dad.
He drank, he fought with Mom.
He left us no food in the fridge.
He got locked up
and never came back.
He seen us but never paid attention.
He heard but didn't care.
I felt like someone threw a fridge at me,
like someone stabbed me in the back of the heart.

Mom asked me a tough question.
Was it better that my father left rather than stayed?
Which is better?
To have a father there who drinks and beats you
or to have no father at all?

When I seen my dad out in the streets,
I tried to talk.
He'd avoid me
and not pay attention.
Me and my dad had a bond.
I used to vent to him all the time.
Now that he's gone and ignores me,
I feel empty
like an empty fridge,
like my heart's been frozen.

Dedicated to my dad and mom

Lonely

I am lonely
like a single human being
left on Earth.
Lonely like a punch to the gut
sucking you into a black hole.

I realize how lonely we all can be,
as if you were by yourself in an old house
with one window,
walking back and forth,
hearing the wood scream with every step.

Lonely is a great summit
of deep, deep feeling.
And from loneliness
I've learned to step forward
out of the lonely shadows
and embrace it
as if it were a friend from the past
and near future.
Lonely.

Dedicated to my family

A Mother Singing

I have a scar on my forehead from him.
I think about him all the time, so let me tell you
all the things I wish he did differently.
I wish that he actually listened to me.
I wish he expressed his anger differently.
He expressed it through drugs and violence
because he has a lot of pain in his heart.
If his heart was a house, it would be black,
the windows would be broken,
the yard would be full of growing trees
and dead plants
because he did try.
I wish he cared about himself more
and that he knew
how much everybody around him cares about him
and loves him.
He can't see that—and he takes the easy way out.
If he actually listened to me,
he would hear the sound of a mother singing.

Dear Dad

When I was younger, and you were deported,
it was really hard for me
seeing them take you out of the house like that
and not knowing what was going on
We were asleep
and a bunch of police in uniforms came in
woke all of us up
took you
and you were gone

I was sitting there crying
wondering
what did you do?
what did I do?
for them to take you away from me

You not being here has really affected me
I see all these other kids with dads
out in the front yard
throwing the ball with them
kicking around a soccer ball
I just wish that you were there with me
I miss you, Dad
I wish that I could have somebody there to talk to
I wish you could've seen me at all my soccer games
I wish you could be there
cheering me on

A Sea of Red

Life's like a bundle of roses.
Some blossom into a beautiful sea of red
grasping every drop of water
through their complex roots
while some become malnourished,
their roots faltering in the soil
until their red shines no more.

The beauty of it all...
Each seed can flourish into excellence
until life is beautiful once more.

Dedicated to everyone struggling to succeed

My Past

I'm thinking about my past,
and how I'm supposed to get out of here.
Just two years ago, I got jumped into a gang.
I started smoking weed, taking drugs.
I became more violent.
I shot two people.
My mom tried to help me get out of it,
help stop my addiction.
I couldn't,
so I ran away.
I ran away into another gang,
and they tried to kill me.
So I stopped going outside.
That's when I stopped going to school
and started fighting more
and selling drugs.

I'm in here now
and I don't know when I'm getting out.
I think about my mom a lot
and what she'd try to tell me.

Thank you, Mom, for being there
when no one else was.
I appreciate everything you do for me
and I want to respect you more.

Thinking of my Mom
is like God watching me all the time.
I can hear her voice sometimes,
a voice like an angel,
smelling like flowers,
tasting like spam musubi.

All I see is a shadow
sitting right next to me.
I wish I could take it all back
but I can't because it's my past.
My past is hell,
smelling like flames.

I wish that my future won't be like my past
and that I'll have a new beginning.
I see stars in my new beginning.
It smells like fresh laundry,
tastes like chocolate,
looks like the universe.

Street Preaching

Thank you for what you gave me
but all of it couldn't save me.
The money kept me alive
but the dope couldn't help people survive.
Pregnant woman itching in her palms,
not ready to be a mom.
She asked him for another rock
before the clock stops.
No matter the age
anybody can get it.

What I gave him
got him on his way to prison.
I could care less
but sitting with him that night
got me thinkin'
if I woulda never sold it to him
would he have another reason?

It's not my fault.
When I heard what happened that night,
I was appalled.
When I heard how much time,
I wasn't broken
but I finally realized
that I was awoken.

The real preachers
are in the house with stained glass windows
and not in a trap with ceilings with holes in it
and not a man handing me a sack
with dope in it.
Trees stay in the ground
and not in a bag.
Rocks are in creeks,
not handed out
and sold in the streets.
Beef is cooked in the kitchen,
not handled with heat
but that's not what they told me.

Gotta Face It

Just some young cats trying to take over the nation.
Kinda hard to uprise
wit all this damn gentrification.
Just 'cause our schools look black,
don't mean they not racist.
Got these standardized tests
that cause education misplacement.
But shit,
I gotta face it—
this the world that I was raised in.
Judges smacking kids wit time,
makin' 'em dry up like some raisins.
Most of my friends don't go to church
'cause it's the streets that they be praisin'.
Parents can't be mad
'cause these the babies they be makin'.
Mom's always working, Pop's hardly seen.
He's like forty
sipping forties on the block,
still sellin' cream.

Dedicated to people in tha struggle

Remembrance

I've had a lot of deaths in my life

My great grandmother
The smell of roses, like her perfume
like grandmothers do

My sister
Her big grin, like when she pranked me
A smile as big as the sun

My uncle
He lived every day like he was going to die the next

My cousin
A big, blue sombrero
Joking that she would join a mariachi band

My mom
The best bear hug ever. She was a pro-wrestler
She wouldn't let you go
and I haven't let her go

If I were to paint a picture with all my deaths
it would be a picture of world peace
The earth with all of them
holding hands in a circle around it

The Way I Am

I've been in and out of jail, in and out of juvie.
I'm getting sent over to prison in a few days.
I've heard a lot of bad stories about that place
but I'll be ok.
There are hard cases there that don't really care.
They get into lots of fights, and they're never fair.
I'm not really worried, I'll just keep my guard up
and know who I'm dealing with.

Honestly, I feel like most of my life
I've been locked up.
Not in jail, but in my head,
not being able to be who I truly am.
I can't reach my full potential
because something's always weighing me down.
It may not be 4 walls
but it can be in the way I think of myself.
Being in a cell is like being a bird in a cage.
When the caged bird sees another bird fly,
it looks like flying is a sickness
'cause the caged bird has never been able to fly,
to see what it's like to be free.
Not being able to call my family,
'cause they were never there for me.
I grew up surrounded by people but alone.
Can you be an orphan when you have parents?

All that I've learned in my life
has been from the streets.

The way I walk
looks like I just don't care
but really it's a bad leg
that makes me look like a pimp.
The way that I am
is a product of my environment—
South Central Los Angeles.
Going to sleep with gunshots in the air,
crack heads on the corner,
seeing dead bodies as a kid...
I saw one out my window,
puddle of blood around his head.
Whenever I heard gunshots
I ran to the window to see what was going on.

The judge calls me a menace to society
but I can't be no other way.
It's what happens when you grow up on the streets
not making a lot of friends,
always getting into trouble.
Inside,
I'm just a good guy
in a bad situation.
I'm gonna keep my head up
like a king not allowing his crown to fall.

Dedicated to my life

Heart

I got court today
I could take it to trial
I could take the deal
and get sent up
I could take it to court
and get some adult time

It's dead silent when I walk in
Everyone seems like they are looking at me
Like they are against me
It feels cold
Unforgiving
Everyone wants me to stay in there longer
like they have cold hearts
Like their heart is coming through their eyes
Their glare is freezing me up
They try to make me seem like I'm a monster
like I have no heart

My heart is a stone
a hardened shell around my body
I want to be out there
I want to have an opportunity to prove myself
They are trying to keep me under the jail
like they are going to bury me
Once the door opens to release me
my heart is an open door

Memories of Me

1. My mom first taking me to school
2. Me going to school by myself in middle school
3. Finding out I have a little brother
4. First day of high school
5. First time getting put on the basketball team
6. Meeting my little brother
7. Going to his first football game
8. Me finding out I'm having a son
9. The first time I bought my son clothes
10. When I first told my mom I was having a kid
11. When she accepted it
12. My mom helping me trying to find myself
13. My mom letting me go and live
14. My son's mother being stressed
and telling her everything will be fine
15. Getting my first job
16. Getting into community college

Dedicated to my family

Hurt

Hurt is a painful thing–
an emotion which comes about
after events happen in your life.
As I remember, I've had hurt
ever since I was about six years old.
I felt the hurt from my mom
when my father would actually hurt her.
I felt the hurt when my sisters
got assaulted in multiple ways by my dad.
I felt the hurtful pain
when drugs took my spot in my father's heart.
I felt the hurt when my dad left
for years upon years.
Hurt is a thing we all feel.
It makes you feel emerged with hate
and thoughts that you wouldn't imagine.
Hurt is a thing—a feeling
that made me who I am today
and it's hurt
I want to thank.

Nobody Knows
My Name

The Fear of Love

Love is a word that easily skims through our lips
Girls cut their wrists, and dudes kill for it

I sit in the county jail cell
I write your name on the wall
With this tonight, I disgrace myself

I speak to you with my soul
but you just stand there staring
and the door's closing

I stay in the street, with no money
Nobody knows my name
and nobody cares

I think about the past to get to my future

I stay paranoid with the fear of losing you
I would lose my life for you
to show my love for you

but I couldn't leave you with no one to love

Dedicated to my family and loved ones

Addiction

I am addicted to the streets.
In my addiction, my life is filled with hatred,
enemies, guns, drugs.
In my addiction, I'm glad to feel hated by many.
I am addicted to the numbness
caused by the substance I ingest
to feel the rage–
the emotion where
the anger I carry explodes within me
splattering, splashing,
breaking, destroying
my soul, my self,
my mind,
ME.

In my addiction,
I think about the damage I caused,
the hearts I broke,
the splinters in my fists.
In my addiction, the real me
becomes an unwanted thing.

I am addicted to being understood,
to be given the chance to express myself
without prejudice.
In my addiction, betrayal comes
in the form of denial. I am addicted.

Killing Me Inside

I'm turning 18, and my brother's not here
This is the first birthday that he's missed
It's killing me inside
that he doesn't get to see me turn 18

There were days where me and him
were doing grown-up things
Smoking weed, buying Swisher sweets
And now I'm finally 18
and I can finally do those grown-up things legally
but I'm scared that he's not here
to take care of me

There's a hole in my heart without him
Being 18 I don't know where to start
Me and my brother were so close
He was half of my heart
Now my other half is gone

I feel really alone now that he's not home
Not in his apartment, with his daughter
stopping by our house to say 'hi'

There's nobody to talk to
about my deepest problems
I used to talk to him about anything
Now I don't know who I can trust with everything

My Frenemy

My best friend
and my worst enemy,
my drug addiction.
It's always there for you.
It's reliable,
especially when you're used to people
not being there for you.
It's something that's fun.
It's something that got me a lot of friends
who had a common thread—
doing it together.
It also got me a lot of enemies.
It makes you a different version of yourself,
a person who doesn't care
that you're robbing people,
that you're screwing over your family,
that you're willing to cheat on your boyfriend.
The appeal is it allows you to become someone—
someone you always wanted to be.
An outgoing person, the life of the party.
But it's a false reality.

Dedicated to struggling addicts

Mamá

Hace siete días que llevo aqui encerrado
por un delito que no ha sido comprobado.

Recuerdo a mi mamita diciendo,
"Hijo te amo, por favor no cometas ningún pecado."

Yo nunca la escuchaba y siempre la ignoraba.
Y ahora me arrepiento.

No sabes como me siento.
Cada vez que mi Corazón late
sale llanto con sentimiento
y tan sólo lo intento cada véz
que respiro el viento.
El aire que me da sustento.

Quisiera devolver el tiempo
para regresar a aquellos días
cuando tu me decías y me aconsejabas
lo Bueno y lo malo que yo negaba.

Mother

It's been seven days since I've been locked up
for an assault that has not been proven.

I remember my sweet mother telling me,
"Son, I love you, please do not commit any sins."

I ignored her, never listened to her.
Today I regret it.

You have no idea how I feel.
Every time my heart beats,
sad tears flow
and with each and every breath I take,
I breathe the same air that sustains me.

I wish I could turn back time
to go back to those days
when you gave me advice
about the good and the bad I denied.

Dedicated to my mom

Translation by RAÚL SANCHEZ

Josiah

You see that I am always getting in trouble
Trouble follows me
like a shadow right behind me, always
You see that I am always in fights
Always rebel fights, arguments
But you don't know me. I'm not that type of person
I'm really caring, giving
Always trying to help people
I try to make other people happy
I put others' happiness before my own

Since 2018, it's been trouble, trouble, trouble
When the new year came, everything changed
When my friend, Josiah
was shot and killed 4 months ago
it changed me

At the funeral, I touched his hands
We drove to the funeral in a white limo
Twenty of us
Josiah looked so nice in his tux
His hair was done, his hands were so cold
He was the first dead body I've ever seen

On December 1, I was at my house
in my room when my friend called and told me
Josiah had been shot, but he was going to be ok
But the next morning
I saw on Snapchat—RIP

I had to call my friend, my brother
to give him the bad news
We both cried for an hour
The funeral was on December 15

I was doing good until Josiah
but after
everything changed
I just stopped caring about anything
I still had to take care of my girlfriend
and my mom
but it was hard
We were so close

Now Josiah's brother is an only child

I turned into another person
I just turned savage
Josiah was the only person we knew who had graduated
had a job, and had something going for him
When he left, it broke me

Lost and Found

Love was lost when my mother passed
like the sun behind the clouds.
So, I took to the streets to fill the gap
like the earth when it cracks.
A young lost soul with no sense of direction
roaming this lonely world
with a heart full of hatred and deception.

Love was lost, love was found.
She became my queen,
she held the crown.
The glow that guided me,
she became the light
to my lonely, darkened world.
A love I lost, a love awoke—
my guiding light.

My Roots

Half of my family is in Mexico
the other half is here
I was born and raised in Seattle
surrounded by tall pine trees, rivers, and mountains
where the sun shines and hides in the winter months
The rain is abundant and keeps everything green
However
I am disconnected from my family in Mexico
They only hear the bad things
but not the good things
They do not know I am an artist
I play the bass like nobody's business
I tried to follow the footsteps of my family
but they don't know that
I got in a fight with my father
My grandmother doesn't like me either
My Spanish isn't that good
but the music in me sings through my fingers
when I play my emotions on the bass
I like the deep tones
The ones deep as the feelings in my heart
I want to say what I feel if they would just listen
But I can always be the artist I already know I am
because I take pride
in the roots deep down in the soil
wherever I walk

Black is Beauty

Bully, aye—
Yes, you—
Why you so black?
Yes, you—
Why you so mean? Why me?
Blacker than black—
Go back home where you came from.
Aye, yes, you are ugly—
and blacker than the blackboard.

Aye, yes, you—
you're so beautiful.
Your skin is so beautiful.
Aye, yes, me.
Is this really you?
A black beautiful young woman.
You should be a model.

Dedicated to my mom

My Backpack of Pain

Reasons to Love Me

1. I may not be perfect,
but I can turn things around like a merry-go-round.

2. I always wish that my life will mean something,
like the point of view of a book.

3. I do my best to understand my surroundings
and events that happen in my life, like a movie.

4. I can create an image of my future
that I believe is possible.

5. I hold onto some things forever,
like the clothes I wear every day
and the pain I carry like a backpack.

6. I have unusual ideas,
like how the world will turn out to be.
Will there be a future?

7. If I were an animal, I'd be a dolphin
so I could swim through the ocean like my mom wanted.

8. I am a great, trustworthy, angry, sad teddy bear.

Dedicated to anyone who's going through it, and my mom

Fresh Air

Freedom tastes like a bowl of wild berry sherbet.
Freedom is the sound of a mockingbird chirping
in a tree swaying in the breeze.
Touching freedom is hugging your mom
without people watching.
Freedom smells like roses blossoming
in the spring sunlight
at a lighthouse on the beach,
waves crashing, birds singing
without a care in the world.

Freedom tastes like a ripe mango on a warm summer day,
refreshingly juicy with the sun beating down.
Freedom is the sound of the phone waking you up
and Mom telling you to get up and go to school.
Touching freedom is like getting your paycheck
after a long week of work.
Freedom smells like wood burning at a campfire
in the middle of the forest, away from civilization
where people can be themselves
without being judged.

When I look at freedom, I see myself
breathing out the stale air of Detention
and breathing in the fresh air of the rainy city.

Lifestyle of Worries

I want to get out of here.
I'm worried about my grandma.
I want to take care of her.
Anything could happen to her right now
with me not there to protect her.
She has been the most important person in my life.
She's been there since I was 2 years old
because my mom and dad lost custody.
It's hard thinking about her.

I'd been seeing my mom about 3 times a month
but she passed away when I was 11 or 10.
It tore me up a little bit.
I feel like my dad.
He's been there a little bit
but he's been in and out of prison my whole life.
I talk to him on the phone sometimes.

Sometimes I feel lonely.
I don't really got nobody on my side
and then when I think about my mom,
tears just come down like a waterfall off a cliff.
When I think about my dad
I want him to be better.
I don't want him to be in prison.

He's supposed to get out soon
and I just hope he stays out of trouble.

I feel so lonely
it's like a dark cloud has wrapped me up.
My worry is like me standing on a cliff
and it's breaking apart
and I'm falling off the edge,
washed away in the waterfall.

I miss my sister.
She's a strong person, focused on school.
When I think about her,
it's as if she has angel wings wrapped around me
and eagle eyes watching.

I feel like God sent me down here
to think about my life, to protect me from death,
to help me get control and find a better path.
And I know when I get out
God is going to protect me,
show me a better life, help me get back in school,
help me protect my grandma and sister.
The man I was meant to be
is a protector of my loved ones.

Five Poems

I

You see that I scream, that I cry.
But you don't know me.

You would know me if
you knew how hard it was to live,
how I feel sometimes that I'm alone,
and how family didn't care.

You see that I cry, that I smoke.
But you don't know me.

You would know me if
you knew how I survive, how I fight—
if you knew how I screamed.

II

My body aches
from the last time
it was broken
into its screams for help
but no one
is listening.

III

I'm cold and lonely.
Please come hold me
till the demons let me go.

IV

I see the rainbow
but there is no color.
I see black and white
just like my heart.

V

She was afraid and crying.
He stood there looking out at her
with evil in his eyes.
He broke her, not only mentally
but also physically
and she can never be fixed.

If I Could Speak

If my fist could speak, it would tell you
I am brave and tough.
If my feet could speak, they would recall
how I run away from violence.
If my eyes could speak, they would tell you
about all the things I have seen.
Like when my family is together, it is beautiful.
If my pounding heart could speak, it would say
how scared I am of seeing people die.
If my hair could speak, it would explain
it is short and beautiful.
If my ears could speak, they would share
all the hate it hears, all around.
If my body could speak, it would tell you about
how strong and beautiful it is.
If my brain could deal with everything,
it would want to ask
why people fight and hate
and why there is so much crime.

Where I Come From

I'm from a street
where most things have to be gotten on your own.
I'm from a faith
where I believe in myself and my family for survival.
I'm from a long line of people
who try to make the best of their situation.
I'm from confusion
about how the world works in different ways.
I'm from laughter
over the difficulties that I made it through in life.
I come from a family that wishes me the best.
I'm from love
and I know that because my family shows me
by telling me what I'm doing wrong.
I'm from fear,
especially when I think about failure
and wasting my life when I can do so much more.
I come from a long line of strong people
like my mother and father.
I come from experiences like the streets
and how bad they can get.
I come from a smart community
that uses their smarts for crime.
And I wish my life
would become better as the days go on
and stronger too.

I Wish

I wish we could have spent more time together
We never expected you to leave us
I wish spending time with you was my main priority
I never expected this to happen to you

I wish you could have taught me how to do graffiti
That you could have met our other nephew
That I could have seen you become a dad
You would have been a great dad

I wish we could go fishing or crabbing
That we could drive around downtown and play music
and scream out the window and tell jokes
I wish we could have had more laughter together

I wish we could watch another football game
so I could clown on you about your team
I wish we could all get together again
Make new memories together and repeat

My Pride/Mi Orgullo

The day I get out of here,
I will change my life around
and live my life in a new light.
I want to become a veterinary doctor.
I love animals, *todos los animales*
especially horses.
I miss our horses, beautiful horses.
The fire killed them all, mysterious fire.

The fire that burns within me
cannot be extinguished easily
because as long as I'm behind these walls,
there isn't much I can do.

When I get out of here,
beyond these cold walls and the stale food,
I will work hard to regain my path
and fulfill my goals.
I know I can because I can do what others can't do
like taming bulls, and horses.
I know all the tricks
such as roping, chasing, galloping,
and my favorite—*manganas!*
I am proud to be Mexican.
I love my culture,
my food, my customs,
our celebrations, my family.

This Is Who You Are to Me

a poem to my mom on her birthday

In my ocean, you are a lionfish
with radiant, colorful spines
because you are beautiful but fierce.

In my grassy field
you are a pathway straight and clear
because you show me the way.

In my galaxy, you are a spaceship flying fast
because you stay on course to great things.

In my body, you are my legs, strong and supportive,
because you're the reason I keep going.

You are my world.

Dedicated to my sister

Pain All My Life

I've been in pain all my life,
fighting to keep my head up.
I keep my head down.

I was born into pain, a baby drowning in pain.
My pain felt like being stabbed,
an open wound that wouldn't heal.
My pain felt like a person yelling for help.
My pain is pinkish, orangish—
sadness like I've been hurt.
My pain felt like being stuck in a hole or a ditch.

I turned to drugs to ease my pain.
At first, I felt relieved, so I started using more.
The pain kept throbbing.
My pain ached like something in a horror movie.
My pain makes me feel like I'm locked up.
It keeps trying to imprison.

I've been fighting the urge.
I think about what happens if I relapse.
I want to go back to school, get a job.
I'll look to positive things instead of negative.
I'll think about where I am now,
and where I could go.

Hula-Hoops of Problems Cycling Around

To Estefani

I'm addicted to the streets,
but I'm tired of knowing my mother cries to sleep.
She wants to see me change,
but I can't find that lane.
My heart is cold as winter snow,
but these people don't really know.
I've been through so much
that my mind thinks it's froze,
losing my friends got me traumatized
'cause I feel like I'm losing all of mine.

I want to make someone proud,
but I don't know how.
I'm stuck in the negative
and don't know how to get out.

I come from where the streets are always wet,
but it's not from the rain.
Blue and red lights passing by—
it's probably another homicide.
A lot of families crying,
'cause their sons and daughters are dying.

I'm from one of those families,
but I didn't die.
I'm just serving a lot of time
but that's the only option
when you're living this life.

If God Were Looking at My Life

He'd wonder why I am where I am.
He'd understand that we made mistakes.
He'd know the way things had gone for me,
gone bad because of my environment.

He'd remember how things went when I was little,
like how I used to think dat was how actual life was
and I was happy.
He'd know that I was innocent and caring,
not just for myself—
like how I'd take ass-whoopings for BB.
He'd know that I'm trying to change certain things,
like this cycle I'm in.

He'd know how hard it was to change
because he's seen this before.
He'd want me to understand that life is not easy.
If God opened a new door for me,
it would lead me to probably heaven.
Then, I could start over with my life.

Dedicated to my siblings

If My Fist Could Speak

If my fist could speak, it would tell you
about fractures and breaks.
If my feet could speak,
they would recall how many miles it takes
to find a safe place to sleep.
If my eyes could speak, they would tell you
about the poverty and crime I see in my city.
If my hair could speak,
it would explain how coarse my life is.
If my ears could speak,
they would share the secrets I've kept to myself.
If my body could speak,
it would tell you about the beating it took
to become stronger.
If my brain could, it would want to ask
why is life so difficult.

Dear Dad

I just thought you should know what I'm doing now.
I am a sad, lonely, depressed, and angry girl
who spends a lot of time doing bad things,
grown things a child shouldn't have to do.
I just thought you should know how I'm feeling.
I am angry, hurt, scared
because I don't have a father or mother
to lead me in the right direction.

Just thought you should know what I've been through.
Since the last time you seen me,
I have grown, suffered,
and maybe even changed to my own lil' person
you don't even know.

I just thought you should know
what I wish for the future.
I hope that you can get out of prison
and step up and be a father.

I just thought you should know
what I don't miss about you.
I'm glad I don't have to worry about you hurting me.

I just thought you should know what I miss a lot.
I miss the way we used to write.
I just thought you should know
that I'm gon' keep it pushing
with or without you.

Addicted

I am addicted.
I am addicted to meth, heroin.
In my addiction, my life is filled
with a bunch of bad people,
drug addicts who want nothing better for themselves.
In my addiction,
I am glad to feel myself getting sober.

I am addicted to older men.
In my addiction, I hate
to think about me liking grown men
'cause I was raped by a man
who should have protected me.

In my addiction, the real me
becomes someone who cries no more.

In my addiction, betrayal
comes in the form of me being left behind.

In my addiction, I struggle to love myself.

I am addicted to school
where I am hiding my intelligence.
In my addiction, I'm in a constant battle
with me thinking I'm not smart.
I am addicted to pain.

I Am Old and New

I feel old when I can't think of new ways to live,
when my problems cycle around me like a hula-hoop.
I feel new when I get out of jail
and my friends look at me different.
I feel old when every staff in Juvenile
knows my name.
I feel new when I meet old friends again.
To be new is impossible
when I get recognized as infamous
instead of celebrated.
To be new
is possible when everybody can invest
wisdom in the new generation.

Running

When i was really little, i ran away from my abusive mom.
i was afraid of getting beat every day, all day.
i dream about becoming a nurse or a counselor
so i can help other kids
'cause my cousins, brother, sister,
never had that love and attention.

When i got a little older, i ran away from my family.
When i ran, i expected that i would find
someone to save me.
At the time, i ran toward the streets.
When i ran, i hoped for help, something good,
but instead, i ran into a gang.

Today when i run, i run away from suicidal thoughts.
More than anything, i wish i could run
from all the hurt that i have.
Today when i run, i run toward being somebody.
More than anything,
i wish i could run to my mom or dad for love.

Dedicated to teenagers like me

I'm Trying to Change Certain Things

If God were looking at my life,
He'd wonder why I make it harder on myself.
He'd know the way things had gone for me—
they've gone left and right, up and down,
across and around.
He'd remember how things went when I was little—
little dreams with low expectations.
He'd know that I was in and out of jails.
He'd know that I'm trying to change certain things
like becoming a better father, brother, and son.
He'd know how hard it is to change
because I am poor and black and young in America.
He'd want me to understand that life is going
to keep going without me.

If God opened a new door for me,
it would lead me to better opportunities.
Then I could start over with my life.

The Lessons of Courage and Fear

In my life, I've known Courage.
We met when I was 11, growing up fast and scared.
Nowadays Courage is guiding me
and making me stronger.
I find Courage when I'm in a bad situation.

In my life, I've known Fear.
We met when I was locked in a room
alone with a man.
These days Fear is always keeping me on the lookout.
Fear finds me when I get around men I don't know.

I've learned that Courage and Fear are different—
When Courage tells me, *it's ok.*
Take one step at a time,
Fear says, *breathe. Leave the past behind.*
Usually, I listen to my gut feelings.
I wish I wasn't so scared, hurt, broken...
I wish all my courage could protect me.

Strength

I can be as strong as a god
ready to take care of your soul.

I can be as strong as the tiger.
Pay attention to my walk around you—
I will brush my fur against you if you are so sweet.

I can be strong in ways you don't expect.
I can be as strong as a brick
able to squish you from hurting me.

My strength can be gentle.
I can be as strong as an angel,
ready to take you home with me.

I can be strong and change the world.
I can be strong and guide others.
I can be strong and won't have to cry.